Brighton Between the Wars

BRIGHTON
Between the Wars

James S. Gray

B. T. BATSFORD LTD LONDON

Frontispiece
1. *Holiday makers enjoy a new
thrill on the giant wheel at the end of
the Palace Pier, 18 April 1938*

First published 1976
Copyright © James S. Gray 1976
Printed by The Pitman Press, Bath
for the publishers B. T. Batsford Ltd
4 Fitzhardinge Street, London W1H 0AH

ISBN 0 7134 3115 6

Contents

page vi   Acknowledgments

vii   Introduction

illustration number 5–16   Sea Front, Promenades, Beaches and Piers

17–23   People

24–34   The Town Centre

35–42   At Work

43–50   The Inner Perimeter

51–56   Notable Events

57–63   Street Widenings and Improvements

64–68   Personalities

69–72   Forgotten Courts and Twittens

73–83   Sports, Pastimes and Entertainment

84–89   The Outlying Areas

90–95   Transport

96–107   Hove

108–117   Housing: Slums and New Housing Development

118–120   Prelude to War

ACKNOWLEDGMENTS
Although many of the photographs reproduced are from the Author's own extensive collection, the book could not have illustrated many facets of life in Brighton during the period without photographs readily made available from other sources. Between the wars the Borough Engineer's and Health Departments of Brighton Corporation took many photographs of streets, courts, and buildings likely to be affected by early changes, of which those used in the book represent but a tiny proportion. In contrast, the many pictures provided by the Librarian, East Sussex County Libraries, are chiefly of people and supply the human interest. The Author and Publishers express their thanks for the permission granted to use these photographs, and they are also indebted to the individuals mentioned below for their valued contributions.

E. Billam for illustration 86; Borough Engineer, Brighton: 26, 27, 32, 34, 43, 45, 47, 58, 61, 108, 112; Leon Choulat: 54; Environmental Health Department, Brighton: 69, 70, 71, 72, 109, 110, 111; Philippe Garner: 7; Eric Holden: 107; The Librarian, East Sussex County Libraries: 6, 8, 9, 12, 17, 18, 19, 21, 22, 36, 38, 39, 40, 41, 42, 44, 55, 56, 63, 65, 66, 67, 68, 74, 79, 80, 81, 83, 94, 100, 102, 106, 118, 119, 120; London News Agency: 76; W. C. Philbrock: 101; Radio Times Hulton Picture Library: 1, 14, 35, 53, 64, 82, 90; John Roberts: 91; Albert Tanner: 75; The Misses Wiles: 2, 3, 23, 92, 97, 98, 99, 117; Clifford H. Walliš: 31.

The remainder of the photographs are from the Author's own collection.

The Author wishes to thank most sincerely, Miss E. Hollingdale, Local History Librarian, Brighton Area Library, for her enthusiastic help in frequently providing for consideration large numbers of photographs, and for arranging for the reproduction of those chosen. Prolonged research for information needed for some of the commentaries, was, for convenience sake, conducted at Hove Area Library. Here, the Author was greatly helped by Mr R. Churchill, Reference Librarian, Miss J. Dale, Mr W. Duke, and Miss S. Nayar, who continually and cheerfully produced from their archives dozens of reels of microfilms of old local newspapers. For this invaluable assistance they are sincerely thanked. Finally, the Author records his appreciation of the work of Mr John Barrow of Hove, in reproducing many of the photographs, and acknowledges the debt he owes to his wife, Daisy, for her tolerant acceptance of the many hours he had to spend on research at the Library, when he might have been sharing her company.

Introduction

BRIGHTON emerged from the Great War physically unscathed but facing many serious problems. These were mainly of her own making; from the turn of the century to 1914 the town had sunk into a shabby lethargy, only slightly relieved by the visits of Edward VII during 1908–1910. Now, with almost 20 years gone, Brighton had still to be dragged into the 20th century. By contrast, neighbouring Hove seemed almost content to remain as she was: with her Sunday morning Church Parade on the Lawns, her private carriages and bath chairs, and her mainly gas-lit streets, she delicately gathered her municipal skirts about her for fear of contamination from raffish Brighton to the east and industrial Portslade to the west.

Put simply, Brighton's problems were fourfold: overcrowding, slum clearance, the need for street widening and for improving the appearance of her shop window, the sea front. The first two were not complementary; clearing the slums would only add to overcrowding. At the 1921 census, with a population of 142,427, Brighton was recorded as being second only to West Ham, in density of people among County Boroughs. The principal streets were much as they had been 50 years before. Probably the most congested was Western Road, that relic of the old "bridle path to Hove". Here, shops built over the gardens of erstwhile private houses had so narrowed the roadway that in places two buses could barely pass each other in safety. West Street, in direct descent from station to sea, was narrow and dingy, redolent of sausage, potato and onions. North Street, although slightly widened in one part, was plagued by an atrocious bottle-neck at Princes Place, which had endured since 1879. There were others, but these three examples will suffice. On Kings Road, the only notable change since the 1886 widening of the promenade had been the building of the Hotel Metropole in 1889/90, though the surface of the roadway had been improved. Further to the east the attractions of the Palace Pier distracted the attention of visitors from noticing the old Aquarium, now sinking into more and more dilapidation.

A daunting prospect, but as often happens, the hour produced the man. Herbert Carden, a war-time Mayor, was a dynamic character, whose vision at times bewildered his fellow councillors. He had that priceless gift of quick decision; while others debated and temporised, he acted. Much of what the Corporation accomplished in these inter-war years resulted from his foresight, initiative and personal drive. Housing had priority. By mid-1919, land had been bought at Moulsecoomb just outside the Borough boundary, and the building of the Council's first large housing estate was started. This was followed in 1922 by the Queens Park estate, between Elm Grove and Freshfield Road. Private enterprise building started slowly, accelerated by the end of the decade and was in full spate during the '30s.

In 1926 a start was made on the widening of Western Road, at the corner of Crown Street. The method adopted in most, though not all cases, was that the Corporation bought properties on the north side, widened the roadway and let the sites on building

leases. Carried out in stages, the widening occupied 10 years. Large stores such as Boots and Wade's were transferred to the old Bon Marche premises, near Spring Street, while they were rebuilding. West Street was tackled, at Burton's corner, in 1928 and the new building line on the west side established; the widenings in North Street took place mainly in the next decade.

It was a few years before much was done to the sea front. In 1924 the old iron, kerbside railings to the south pavement were removed; then the enclosures to the west of the West Pier were replaced by the boating pool, putting green and sunken gardens. In 1928 the Aquarium was reconstructed and the Sun Terrace added; a year or two later the pavement fronting Grand Junction Road was extended seawards. This extension continued to beyond the Palace Pier and caused Volk's Railway terminus to be moved from adjoining the Pier to its present location. During the '30s the asphalt on the south pavement was replaced by coloured paving blocks, and the lower esplanade improvement continued with the construction of the children's pool and adjoining lawn.

Probably the outstanding event of the 1920's was the extension of the area of Brighton Borough from 2620 to 12,565 acres. There were several reasons for this. Brighton had been forced to go outside its boundaries for land on which to build housing estates. Over the years the town had purchased areas of downland for preservation – Herbert Carden had bought the Dyke Estate from his own resources to forestall development, and resold it to the

3. Arrival of the tank "Hova" in Hove Park, 23 September 1919. Technically known as a Mark IV Female, it was in action at Messines and Arras, and was presented to the town by the Army Council. Disposed of as scrap metal about 1937

4. *Mystery Towers at Southwick, 1919.*
Whatever their use was intended to
be, the end of the War caused work
on them to cease. One was later towed
away to Spithead and is now the Nab
Tower. The other was dismantled
where it lay in 1923

Corporation at the same price. Sporadic development of a poor standard was taking place around the periphery, which Brighton could control when the area was absorbed. Accordingly a Charter was obtained, operative from 1 April 1928. The effect was to bring within the Borough the outlying areas of Rottingdean, Ovingdean, Woodingdean and parts of Saltdean and Patcham. This brought liabilities as well as benefits. Road making and the introduction of essential services were imperative at Woodingdean, while it soon became necessary to widen the coast road to Rottingdean and undertake sea defence works.

Meanwhile, Hove, beset only by overcrowding in its poorer areas, was concerned to repel the advances made by Brighton for amalgamation of the towns. Union with Brighton—Oh dear, no! At this period, with rates at 6/8d in the pound, Hove was the lowest-rated non-County Borough in England. In 1921/22 Hove's first Council houses, in two sections of 33 and 30, were built on the Portland Road estate in spite of criticism from the wealthy and middle-classes, who righteously declared that Hove's artisans should be housed in Brighton or Portslade! From this modest start, Hove continued Council building in her quiet, unspectacular way, on the Portland Road, Old Shoreham Road, and Knoll estates until a halt was called in 1935. Like Brighton, Hove had extended its area, taking in Hangleton and West Blatchington, and was content to let the private builders satisfy all other housing needs, which they were quick to do, particularly along Kingsway and New Church Road.

The "Roaring Twenties" were late in reaching Brighton, but by 1924 Sherrys and Regent Ballrooms were packed each afternoon and evening, seven days a week, with dancers of all ages from seventeen to seventy. With five theatres, about a dozen cinemas, summer bands on both piers, and for a brief period a Municipal Orchestra, there were entertainments to suit all tastes. Later came the Greyhound Stadium and the Ice Rink. Sussex County Cricket

Club, with headquarters at Hove, finished second in the County Championship in successive years 1932, 1933 and 1934. Great days, too, at the Goldstone Ground as during 20 inter-war seasons of football the Albion beat no less than seven Division I teams in the F.A. Cup, a feat they have never once accomplished in post-war football.

But all was not just fun and amusement. Times were hard, wages low and poverty abounded, not only in the slums but also on the distant Council estates, where money spent on food was reduced because of relatively high rents and fares to and from men's work. The Southover Street Canteen, serving a hot meal for 5d and a bowl of soup for 1d, with a later one at Whitehawk, were of great help to the poor and unemployed. For example, Southover Street served 24,000 portions from December 1924 to May 1925.

I have left much unsaid. I have done scant justice to private enterprise, to the builders of the many large private housing estates, to the entrepreneurs who provided six large new cinemas during the period. I have not mentioned the new schools, the extensions to the hospitals, the new parks, the railway or the transport system. The photographs make up for some of these omissions. They reflect some facets of life in Brighton and Hove during these 20 years, alternating topography with people and events.

The inter-war period is still too recent to be judged dispassionately, particularly by one who lived in Brighton through 16 of the 20 years. An historian, 50 years hence, will see the town during these years in much clearer perspective. However, viewing the scene as objectively as I can, this was a period of great change, at times of almost non-stop change. The physical changes are recorded in the photographs; probably in no other comparable term of years was so much accomplished, some of it detrimental but most of it beneficial. But there was a more subtle, less perceptible change taking place, that in the character of the town itself. Still the Mecca of the day tripper, Brighton was losing some of its regular holiday trade to the quieter resorts such as Bournemouth and Torquay. Not that this worried the ever-increasing residential population. They had the sea, the piers, the Downs, the theatres, the cinemas and the dance halls. Yes, Brighton was truly a joyous town in which to live!

James S. Gray.
May, 1975.

Sea Front, Promenades, Beaches and Piers

Previous page
5. *Watching the operation of the newly-installed semaphore traffic signal device, at the foot of West Street, in December 1927. A policeman stood on a raised, enclosed platform and controlled traffic by signal arms operated electrically*

6. *Holiday crowds and Dodgem Cars on the West Pier, Easter Monday, 10 April 1939*

7. A wet Bank Holiday, 7 August 1922. Note the long line of motor-coaches, Volk's Railway Terminus on its original site and the old Aquarium, reconstructed in 1928/29. Also the milkman with barrow, churn and cans

8. *The beach and Kings Road, from West Street to the Queens Hotel, in the summer of 1927. Prominent in the background, the west facade of the Town Hall*

9. *Children from South London, on a day's outing to Brighton, about to disembark after a sea trip in "Skylark" No. 4, 27 July 1939*

10. *The Bank Holiday scene on the beach immediately to the east of Palace Pier, 3 August 1931*

11.   All hands to the capstan to winch up the boats, July 1934. The Palace Pier is in the background

12.   On 22 May 1935 two fishermen brought in this carcase of a 20-foot whale. While they were deciding what to do with it, the tide went out and it was left high and dry on the beach. It was later removed by lorry to the Corporation Depot for destruction

13. The cliffs at Black Rock, 1920, showing Volk's Railway Terminus adjoining the Corporation yard, later the site of the open-air Bathing Pool. This area is now on the fringe of the vast Marina complex

Next page
14. Taking tea in the cafe at the far end of the Palace Pier, 12 August 1939

15. Two forms of transport in Grand Junction Road, with Old Steine and Marine Parade in the background, August 1934. By 1937 only one licensed horse cab remained

16. Volk's Railway Car crossing the crowded beach by the Banjo Groyne, 1935. This particularly well-screened beach was floodlit at night. One of the lamps can be seen against the wall background

People

Previous page
17. *Frances Day, musical comedy and film star, with Sir Harry Preston at the fête in the grounds of Lady Chichester Hospital, Hove, on 26 June 1935*

18. *Dame Elizabeth Cadbury with the Mayoress of Brighton, Mrs John Routley, at the Annual Meeting of Brighton Girls Club in the Royal Pavilion, 4 March 1937*

19. *Fishing for tadpoles at Falmer Pond, 1938*

20. The shopping scene in Kensington Gardens as seen from wood-blocked North Road, in 1923. Trams then ran up North Road to Brighton Station

21. A social chat with drinks at the Reception preceding the Banquet of Hove Arts Club at the Dudley Hotel, Hove, on 1 February 1938

22. *Old folk in a motor-coach outside the Royal Pavilion on 25 August 1936. They were about to leave for their summer outing to Wannock Glen*

23. *A group of boys, the Master and Matron, at the Orphan Boys Home in Upper Lewes Road, 1919. The purpose was "to shelter, feed and clothe orphan boys; to educate them in the Scriptures and general knowledge, to qualify them to earn an honest livelihood". Payment £15 a year!*

The Town Centre

Previous page
24. West Street, 1925. Seen from
Kings Road, it was a narrow dingy
street, about half its present width.
All the buildings on the left side of the
street, except St Paul's Church, have
since been removed

25. West Street, 1925. The view down
the street from the Clock Tower
pavement. The widening of West
Street started here in 1928

26. Looking up North Street from
the corner of Ship Street, 1930. The
building threatened with demolition
is still there 46 years later, but all
those seen on the opposite side have
been removed and the roadway
doubled in width

27. North Street. On this plum, central site at the corner of Princes Place, Braybons Ltd built this show house to advertise their Bevendean Estate. It was here from November 1932 until July 1934, during which time about a quarter of a million people inspected the house

28. The interior of the Floral Hall, 1929. This was built in 1900, part of the building housing the Wholesale Vegetable Market. It extended from Market Street to Black Lion Street. Now the site is used as a car park

29. North Street. Removal of this part of the Royal Colonnade (built in 1823) was carried out on Saturday and Sunday, 29/30 June 1929

30. Few Brightonians could have known of the existence of this cottage, photographed in 1930. It was one of three, numbered 101, 102, and 103, North Street, hidden from view by other buildings. Adjoining Haselgrove's Forge, it was approached by a narrow entry from Regent Row

31. Middle Street. The extensive premises of R. Fry and Co. Ltd, which faced Brighton Hippodrome, and which went back almost as far as West Street. In 1930 the firm moved to new premises at Portslade, and these buildings were demolished to be replaced by a large garage

32. A glimpse of old Market Street, 15 March 1928. To the right was Market Lane, leading to the Thatched House Inn through which existed the old fishermen's right-of-way. The buildings were demolished in 1939

Below
33. Old Steine, looking north, in 1927. Although one-way traffic (north to south) was introduced here in 1926, the trams were excepted and for three more years, until 5 May 1929, they were driven against the general traffic flow

Next page
34. The start of the demolition of Brills Baths, January 1929. This was a circular sea-water bath, constructed in 1869, which occupied a large site between East Street, Pool Valley and Grand Junction Road. The Cinema which replaced it was opened on 1 August 1930

At Work

Previous page
35. A 1930's photograph of Mr Woolgar, Bathing Machine Proprietor, supplying costume, towel and beach shoes to a lady patron. His machines were sited close to the Hove boundary

36. Chestnut seller, 20 October 1934. His pitch, at the corner of Church Street and Regent Street, was well chosen, being very close to the Theatre Royal and the Court Cinema

37. Fish salesman with stall, at the Market on the Level, 1924

38. Milkman steering his milk pram up the steep incline of Trafalgar Street, 29 January 1938. As a self-propelled vehicle this had to carry L plates until the dairyman passed his "test of competence to drive"

39. Hedgecutting at Falmer Road, Woodingdean, 15 January 1938

40. Gypsies at work by the roadside at Pyecombe, 30 April 1938

41. *Unemployed demonstrators halt the traffic in busy Western Road, outside Brighton Labour Exchange, 4 January 1939. Registered unemployed in Brighton and Hove then totalled 7,000*

42. *Policeman removing one demonstrator, who had sat down in front of a bus. He was taken to the Police Station but was later released without being charged*

The Inner Perimeter

Previous page
43. Old shops, 1 to 9, Western Road, on the south side, 1930. A century earlier they had been built in the back gardens of houses in Grenville Place. Demolished in 1967 for the Churchill Square complex

44. In order that Gloucester Place and the foot of North Road could be widened to improve traffic flow, these elegant houses, 1/4, Gloucester Place, had to be sacrificed. Demolition in progress, 10 January 1935

45. Western Road. Boots Christmas Sale, 1926. Soon afterwards these old buildings, originally private houses but occupied by Boots since 1902, were demolished for rebuilding. The present store, on the same site, was opened on 29 November 1928

46. A 1924 photograph of the narrowest part of old Western Road, looking west near Marlborough Street. This stretch of the road was known familiarly as the "Dawkins Dardenelles"

47. Western Road. Imperial Arcade, 1931, built in 1923 on the cleared site of Smithers Brewery, and replaced by the present Arcade in 1934

48. The Open Market on the Level in 1922, looking towards Ditchling Road. The Market started in Oxford Street in 1919. After moves to the Level and the Market Hall in Ann Street, a permanent site was found in Marshall's Row, where the Market opened on 19 October 1926

49. *Marshall's Row, from the London Road end, in 1924. These cottages were built in the 1750's by John Marshall (the end stone bore the date 1754) in the area known as the North Butts, about half-a-mile distant from the houses of Brighthelmston. They were removed in 1938*

50. *17 and 18, Marlborough Place, about 1930. Eighteenth-century cottages, with steps leading down from pavement level, they then formed part of old North Row, at the northern extremity of the town. Demolished in 1935, when the site was redeveloped*

Notable Events

Previous page
51. *Narrow shabby North Street festooned in late April for the celebration of the Silver Jubilee of King George V on Monday, 6 May 1935*

52. *The Prince of Wales at the Unveiling and Dedication of the Chattri, high on the Downs above Patcham, 1 February 1921. Beneath the three granite slabs lie the blocks on which the bodies of Hindu and Sikh soldiers had been cremated*

53. *Brighton was visited by the Duke and Duchess of York (later King George VI and Queen Elizabeth) on 31 May 1928. Among other functions, they opened the new wing of the Children's Hospital, Dyke Road, and are here seen entering their Crossley car in Clifton Hill*

54. *Procession of decorated floats and trade vehicles on Madeira Drive, during the Brighton Carnival of 1923. This was held from Wednesday to Saturday, 13/16 June*

55. *The Proclamation of the Accession of King Edward VIII, from the balcony of Royal York Buildings, on 22 January 1936*

Next page
56. *In Britain for the Coronation of King George VI, this Indian Contingent came to Brighton on 23 May 1937. They are seen outside the Royal Pavilion, where some of them may well have been nursed when wounded during the War. They also visited the Chattri*

Street Widenings and Improvements

Previous page
57. In 1924, Brighton Corporation formed Junction Road by removing the Terminus Hotel, Queens Road and licensed premises in Surrey Street. Ten years later this narrow link road could not cope with increased traffic; early in 1935 work started on this extension

Bottom
59. Work proceeding on the new Marks and Spencer store in Western Road, March 1931. This was the rear view in Regent Row, with Regent Hill in the background. The inn just visible (right) was the Lath Cleavers Arms

58. Western Road, 1930, showing the road widened between Crown Street and Spring Street. The widening had started at Staffords corner in 1926. Wade's were temporarily in the old Bon Marché premises

60. Demolitions at the extreme eastern end of Western Road, 1934. The long glass roof of Imperial Arcade is clearly seen. With the removal in 1967 of many of the buildings on the left, the present roadway here is about three times this width

61. Widening of West Street started at the top in 1928; by 6 April 1931 it had extended about one-third down to opposite the Academy Cinema. Tobacco was then $7\frac{1}{2}$d, $9\frac{1}{2}$d and 11d an ounce!

62.   When Brighton Corporation
decided to construct a War Memorial
they chose a site on the Steine,
occupied by Chantrey's statue of
George IV, erected in 1828. Here, on
14 March 1922, the statue and its
base, weighing 30 tons, is starting
on its short journey to Church Street,
where it stands to-day

63.   On 24 September 1938 North
Street was being more than doubled
in width, between Windsor Street and
Portland Street. On the cleared site
was built the Imperial Theatre

Personalities

Previous page
64. *Jack Dempsey, Heavyweight Champion of the World, with Harry Preston, outside Royal Albion Hotel, 29 June 1925. Davy Burnaby of the Co-optimists takes a cine film. Dempsey spent a week in Brighton and boxed in the Charity Show at the Dome on 4 July*

65. *The Duke and Duchess of Norfolk at Brighton Races, 7 August 1937*

66. *On Monday, 3 January 1938, Anna Neagle and Anton Walbrook made personal appearances at the Odeon Cinema, West Street. They were the stars of the film,* Victoria the Great, *then being screened*

Opposite
67. *Brighton's own comedian, Max Miller, at Brighton Spring Races, 26 June 1937*

68. *Ralph Lynn, watched by Jack Buchanan, laying one of the foundation stones of the Imperial Theatre, North Street, 28 July 1939. The other stone, further east, was laid by Jack Buchanan*

Forgotten Courts and Twittens

Previous page
69. *GERARDS COURT. A cluster of 12 early nineteenth-century cottages, with a narrow entrance from King Street (left) and an exit to Church Street (right). Demolished in 1936. The cleared area is still used as a car-park*

70. *HAYLLARS COTTAGES. These ten whitewashed cottages formed a quiet oasis between busy Middle Street and West Street. Their name came from Daniel Hayllar, a carpenter, who lived at 19, Middle Street (centre) under which was the narrow entrance-way. Removed in 1935*

71. *WILLOW COTTAGES. January 1935. Between 72 and 73, West Street was a passage only three feet wide, ignored by the thousands hurrying down to the sea. It led to three cottages forming three sides of a square. Although the site was cleared 40 years ago, the blocked-off entrance to the passage can still be found*

72. *RUSSELL PLACE. Consisting of 12 cottages of flint and boulder construction, built about 1826, this extended from Russell Street to St. Paul's Church. The back yards were only five feet deep. After their removal in 1936, part of the cleared site was added to the playground of St Paul's School*

Sports, Pastimes and Entertainment

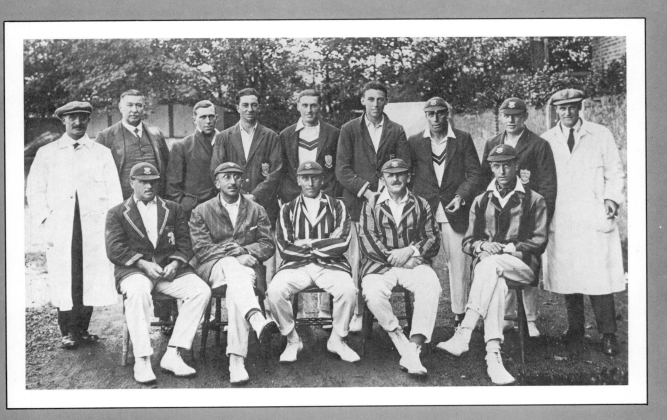

Previous page

73. *Sussex County Cricket Team of 1922, at the County Ground, Hove. Older cricket enthusiasts will recognise and recall these players, notably A. E. R. Gilligan, who captained England in Australia (1924/5), Tommy Cook, and the legendary Maurice Tate*

74. *Brighton, nil – Rosslyn Park, 16 points. This match, at Preston Park on Wednesday, 8 March 1939 was to celebrate 70 years existence of the Brighton Club. It was followed by a Banquet and Dance at the Royal Pavilion*

Right
75. *Not one "bovver boy" amongst these stolid, passive spectators at the Goldstone Ground on 13 January 1923, when Brighton & Hove Albion drew 1–1 with the famous Corinthians in the F.A. Cup. Andy Neil scored for Albion and F. N. S. Creek for Corinthians. Attendance 23,642. Receipts £1,923.*

Right, below
76. *Stan Webb, Albion's goalkeeper, in action against West Ham United in the 5th Round F. A. Cup-tie, at the Goldstone, 18 February 1933. Harry Marsden (left) and Reg Wilkinson (centre) watch anxiously. The result was a 2–2 draw. The attendance of 32,310 remained the Albion record for 25 years, until the Fulham game on 27 December 1958*

ALBION v CORINTHIANS-CUP TIE-1923.

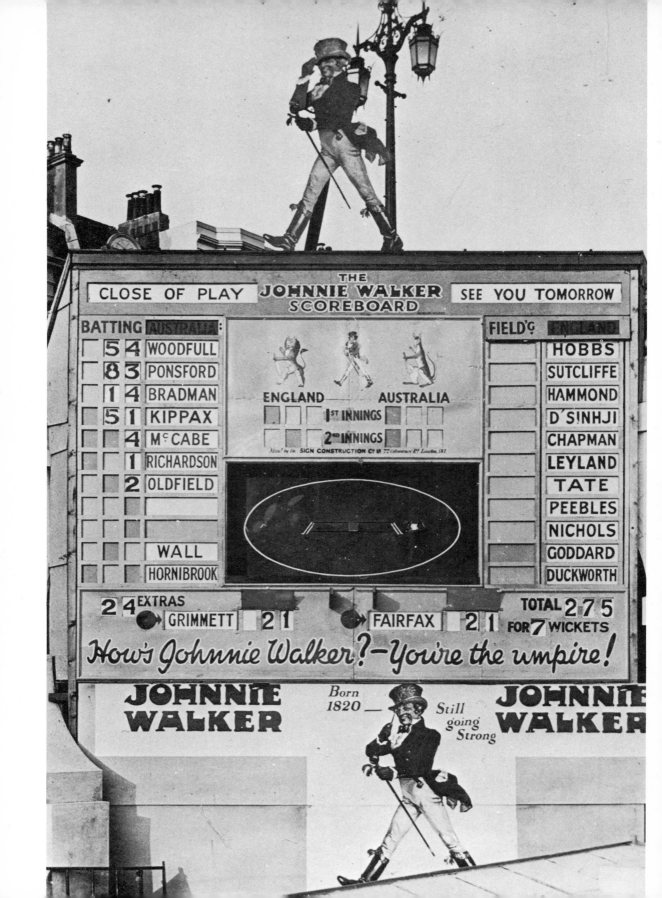

Opposite
77. *In 1930, cricket lovers stood for hours watching the progress of Test Matches on this scoreboard, mounted on the Aquarium Sun Terrace. The location of each ball bowled was shown in the circle representing the field of play. Close of play, first day, fourth Test Match at Manchester, 25 July 1930*

78. *S.S. Brighton, West Street, a splendid new swimming pool, was opened by Commodore Earl Howe, C.B.E., on 29 June 1934. Bathing hours were from 8 a.m. to 10 p.m. However, it was soon converted to an ice-rink, skating starting on 16 October 1935, and never reverted to its original use. Demolished in 1966*

79. *Classical Dancing display at Roedean School, 11 June 1937 – a glorious day. The girls were dressed in primrose, apricot and glowing red, so that "the picture presented glowed like a jewel"*

80. Bathing Belles of 1936. Finalists awaiting adjudication during the Palace Pier Carnival on 8 August. 18,332 people passed through the Pier turnstiles on that day

81. S. R. D'Arcy winning the Stock Exchange, London to Brighton Walk on 2 May 1936. His time was 9 hours, 11 minutes and 34 seconds

82.   The Race Night Ball at Regent
Dance Hall, 23 June 1924. A novel
three-legged race, or one-step, was
held. Jockey Brownie Carslake and
Harry Preston are tying together the
dancers' legs. This famous Ballroom,
known to thousands the world over,
opened on 10 December 1923 and
closed on 30 June 1967

83.   The "Milner Tigers" emulate the
famous Brighton Tigers, of Ice-hockey
fame. The boys played on the asphalt
surface at the back of Milner Flats,
with old sticks and jerseys donated by
Ice-hockey players, and nets from the
fishermen on the beach. 23 February
1939

The Outlying Areas

Previous page
84. *ROTTINGDEAN. The beach and steps, 1929*

Below
85. *ROTTINGDEAN. An aerial view of the quiet unspoiled village in 1921. Beyond, the coast road passed little other than the Coastguard Cottages at Saltdean*

Bottom
86. *WOODINGDEAN. Filling bins and churns with water at the stand pipe opposite the Downs Hotel, in 1926. It was then conveyed by donkey cart to outlying roads, such as the Ridgeway and Crescent Drive, which were entirely without water. The charge is said to have been 6d for five gallons. The Hotel was opened on 7 September 1925*

Right
87. *ROTTINGDEAN. The Midget Stores, 7, High Street about 1930. This was south of West Street and was removed, with adjoining buildings in 1937*

88. WOODINGDEAN. Crescent Drive North at the junction with Downs Valley Road. Putting in mains water pipes in 1929. After its incorporation with Brighton in 1928, all essential services were installed in this, then remote, estate

89. PATCHAM. An old thatched cottage at the foot of Church Hill, close to Patcham House, later the Black Lion Hotel. The photograph is pre-1914, but the cottage was here throughout the inter-war years. Lock-up garages now occupy the site

Transport

Previous page
90. On 29 June 1934, the Southern Belle (all-Pullman train) which had run regularly since November 1908, was renamed the Brighton Belle. On arrival at Brighton Station it was greeted by the Mayor, Councillor Miss Margaret Hardy, M.B.E.

91. Tilling's solid-tyred bus at its terminus in Surrey Street, near the Station, September 1920. The buildings obscured by the bus are those removed in 1924, when Junction Road was formed. The No. 6 route, although much extended, still runs from Brighton Station to Portslade

Right
92. A parade of horse cabs and carriages in George Street, Hove, in aid of charities, in the early 1920's. The Royal George Inn, formerly a private house, was reconstructed and enlarged in 1924

93. Tamplin's drays, horses and drivers paraded in the Brewery yard, August 1934. Soon afterwards the horse-drawn drays were replaced by motor vehicles

94. *Inauguration of the Shoreham-Jersey Air Service, 31 May 1937. The four-engined De Havilland biplane, operated by Jersey Airways Ltd flew the 150 miles in 75 minutes*

95. *Trams at the Old Steine Terminus, 1925. Introduced in 1901 the Tramway system served seven routes, at very cheap fares. During 1939, they were gradually superseded by Trolley Buses; the last tram ran, on the Queens Park route, on 1 September 1939*

Hove

CHURCH RD & HOVE TOWN HALL.

Previous page
96. Church Road, looking west in 1921. The 1882 Town Hall, designed by Alfred Waterhouse, was destroyed by fire on 1 January 1966, while the mansion, 2, The Drive, (extreme right) was later reconstructed for business use, and the pavement widened

Right
99. A crowded beach scene, Summer 1919

100. Punch and Judy show on the beach in front of the lawn near Hove Street

97. Beach chalets, 1919 style. These were on the West Hove beach, not far from Hove Seaside Villas, seen in the background

98. The climax of Hove Baby Week in 1920, came on Saturday, 3 July, when this "pram parade" seen in George Street journeyed from Clarendon Villas Hall to St Anns Well Gardens, for the presentation of the prizes won at the Baby Show

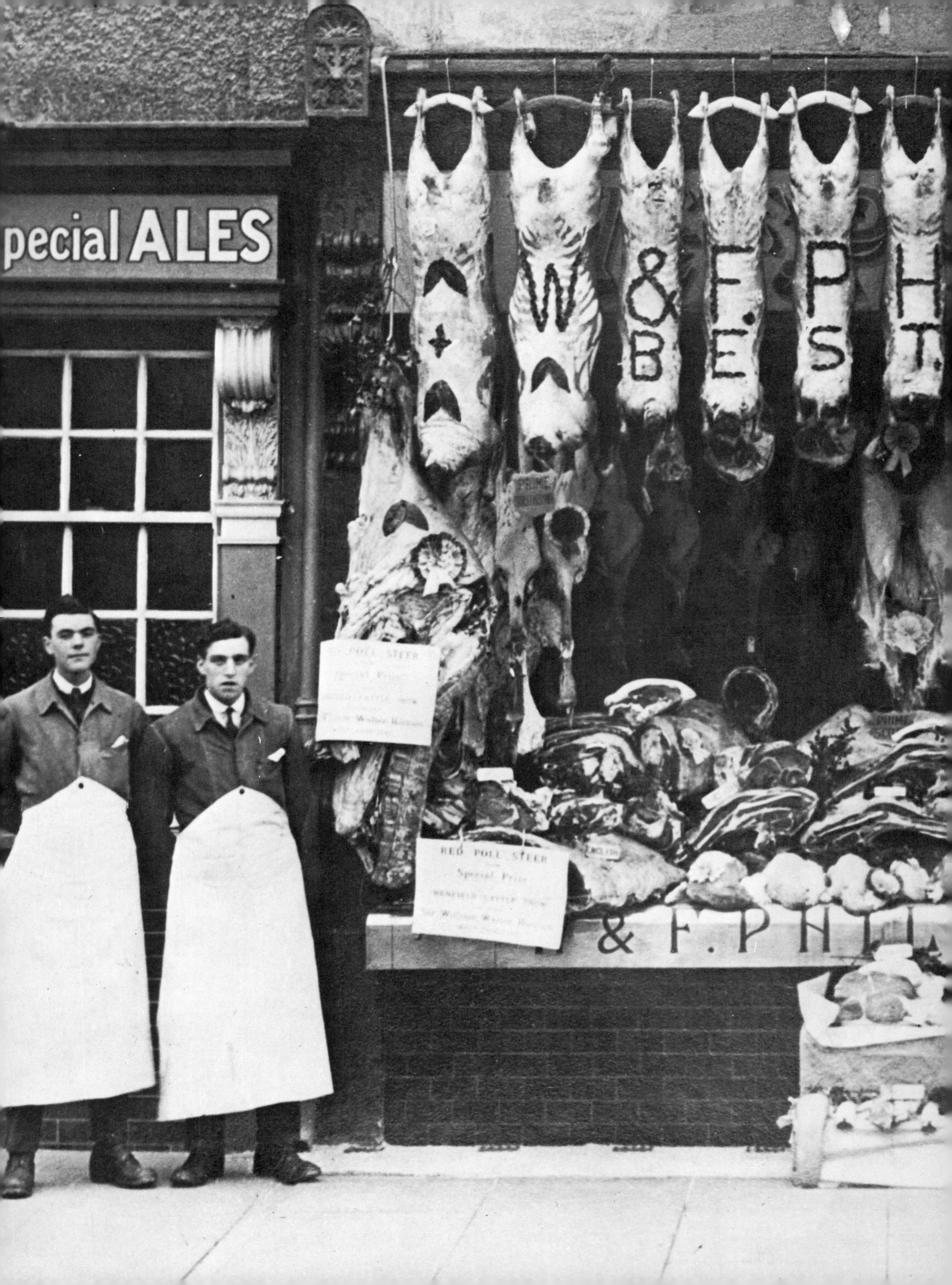
pecial ALES
W & F. P H
B E S T
RED POLL STEER
Special Prize
& F. P H I L

RED POLL STEER
Special Prize
BENEFIELD CATTLE SHOW
Sir William Walter Hornum

RED POLL STEER
Special Prize
BENEFIELD CATTLE SHOW
Sir William Walter Hornum

Previous page
101. *An appetising display at Philbrock's, 11, Victoria Terrace in 1922. One of the oldest-established Butcher's shops in Hove, dating from the 1850's, its original address was 7, Albert Terrace, so named after the Prince Consort*

102. *July 1937. Hangleton Church in its rural setting, with the advancing tide of houses still about half a mile distant*

103. *Gibbets Farm, so named from the gibbet which formerly stood just north of Old Shoreham Road. The farm was given up in 1930. Samuel Holmes, the last farmer, gave his name to Holmes Avenue, which with Elm Drive and the adjoining roads, now occupies this site*

104. West Blatchington Mill, farm buildings and pond in 1920 when this was a remote hamlet, well outside the Borough Boundaries. On 3 May 1936 barns at the base of the mill were destroyed by fire and the farm was given up. In 1937 Hove Corporation bought five acres of land including the mill, to ensure its preservation

105. Listening to the band at Western Lawns Bandstand was a popular pastime of the 'twenties, though the prevailing south-west wind could be troublesome. To mitigate the effect of this the cast-iron, glazed windscreen was built in 1924/5. The bandstand was removed in 1965

106. *Aircraft crash at Lyndhurst corner. On 24 January 1938, a single-seater Bristol fighter, one of four on a formation flight from Kenley, got out of control and crashed. The pilot landed by parachute in Beaconsfield Road, Brighton, his only injuries being bruises and a cut tongue*

107. *Sackville Road, September 1926. This brick arch was built in 1840 to carry the Brighton-Shoreham Railway across the narrow Hove Drove, then just a country lane. By the 'twenties, it had become a serious obstruction, buses having to terminate at Coleridge Street. Its removal and replacement by the present girder bridge in May 1927 led to the opening up of the large area above Old Shoreham Road, with consequent, rapid development*

Housing:
Slums and New Housing Development

THE SLUMS

Previous page

108.   Claremont Row, looking south
from Richmond Street, 1935; the
houses were demolished in the following
year. On the right was Richmond
Street School, built in 1872 and removed
in 1962. The site is approximately
that of the Ashton Rise Flats

109.   Manchester Row, a dead-end
alley, had its entrance at 36, Upper
Bedford Street. Behind it, separated by
only seven feet were the backs of
ancient houses in Crescent Cottages.
In April 1919 Brighton Corporation
paid £1,125 for 31 of these dwellings,
an average price of £35 each.
Manchester Row was cleared in 1925

110.   Houses on the north side of
Hereford Street in December 1924,
shortly before their demolition. The
poles and lines were for hanging out
the washing since there was no room
at the back. On the cleared area,
and that of Paradise Street to the rear,
were built 20 Council houses, some of
which still remain

111. 1928. This entrance from 10, Carlton Hill, just six feet wide, gave access to Carlton Court. Here were 15 ancient cottages, one of which was sold in 1926 for £50! Many were of flint and brick construction. Carlton Court was demolished in 1933

112. The gaunt appearance of hilly Sussex Street, with side roads, Woburn Place and Nelson Row, in 1932. The central building was a Mission Hall. Part of this site is now occupied by Kingswood Flats, built in 1938, and named after Sir Kingsley Wood, Minister of Health in the Chamberlain Government

113. In this panoramic view, from the Municipal Hospital about 1936, the houses in the immediate foreground are on the Queens Park Council Estate. Consisting of about 500 houses, this was the Corporation's second post-war housing undertaking and occupied the years 1922–1925

114/5. Houses under construction in Ladies Mile Road, formerly a narrow drove road, in 1932. These were among the first to be built on this large estate at Patcham, comprising some 850 houses. The advertisement for this estate was displayed in nearby Old London Road

116. *Brighton's first high-rise flats, seen from the sunken gardens in August 1935. Embassy Court, which brought a new dimension to Brighton's sea front, was built on the site of Western House, an elegant mansion demolished in 1930. Advertised rents ranged from £160 to £500 per annum*

117. *Hove's first Council houses, 2/8 and 10/16, Ingram Crescent, in 1922. The initial phase of 63 units was built under the Housing and Town Planning Act, 1919, often known as the "Assisted Scheme" or the "Addison Scheme". Rents of these flats were 8/6d a week and of the non-parlour houses 10/9d, both exclusive of rates. These buildings were demolished in 1974 as part of comprehensive redevelopment*

Prelude to War

Previous page
118. Child evacuees from London meeting their hosts at their temporary home in the Brangwyn area, 1 September 1939

119. Territorial Army call-up. Men of the Royal Engineers assembled outside the Drill Hall in Queen Square on that fateful Saturday, 2 September 1939

120. Recruits of the newly formed 70th (Sussex) Searchlight Regiment, R.A., (T.A.) watching a demonstration at their H.Q. at Highcroft, Dyke Road, on 15 December 1938. The unit was embodied on 24 August 1939